KING'S MEN AT MACKINAC:

The British Garrisons, 1780 - 1796

by

Brian Leigh Dunnigan

Illustrated by Dirk Gringhuis

Reports in Mackinac History and Archaeology
Number 3
MACKINAC STATE HISTORIC PARKS
© 1973
First Printing 1973, 3000 copies
Second Printing 1984, 2000 copies
Third Printing 1993, 3000 copies

ISBN-0-911872-19-1

Printed by Harlo Printing Co.
Detroit, Michigan 48203

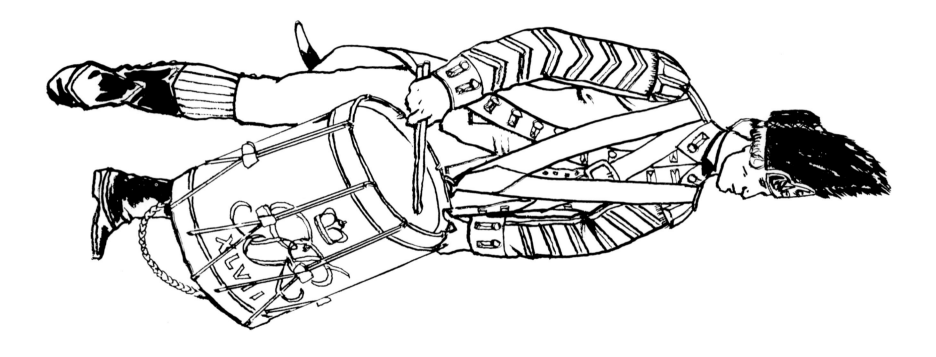

Contents

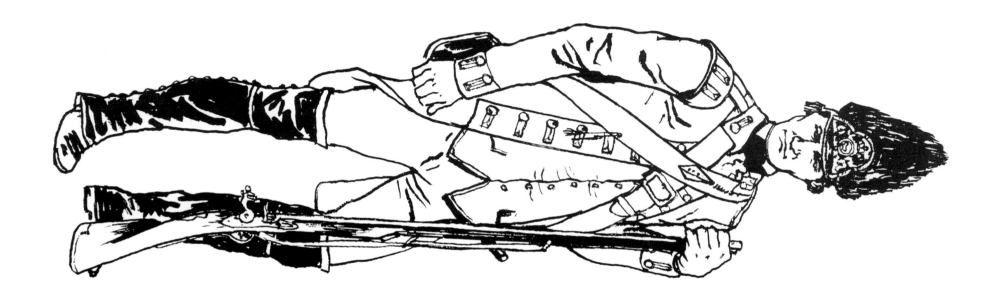

THE BRITISH ARMY IN THE UPPER GREAT LAKES 1780-1796

The end of the French and Indian War in 1760 found the British masters of virtually all of North America east of the Mississippi River, including the vast, former French possession of Canada. The vital fur trade of Canada and the Great Lakes also came under English control and, along with it, the need to regulate and protect the men who engaged in this trade. The English, like the French before them, maintained a string of garrisoned military posts scattered along the line of the five Great Lakes. From these isolated posts, a watchful eye was kept on the Indians, the local traders and, later, the Americans to the south. A major uprising of the Great Lakes Indians in 1763 had temporarily driven out or destroyed most of the small garrisons although the larger posts of Detroit and Niagara had been held. When British control

was re-established in 1764, many of the smaller forts were not re-occupied and the garrisons were concentrated at the more major posts. During and after the American Revolution, the British Army garrisoned the Great Lakes posts of Carleton Island (at the eastern end of Lake Ontario), Fort Ontario (Oswego, New York), Fort Niagara (Youngstown, New York), Fort Schlosser (above Niagara Falls), Fort Erie (Fort Erie, Ontario), Detroit and Michilimackinac (at Mackinaw City until 1780-81 and on Mackinac Island after this date). Later in the 1790's, posts were established at Kingston (Ontario) and Fort Miamis (on the Maumee River in Ohio).

The role of the Great Lakes posts during the American Revolution was not a passive one. Forts Ontario and Niagara were staging points for Indian and Loyalist raids into Western New York, and Detroit sent many raiding parties into Kentucky and the Illinois country. Mackinac supported Detroit and also sent raids against the Illinois, and

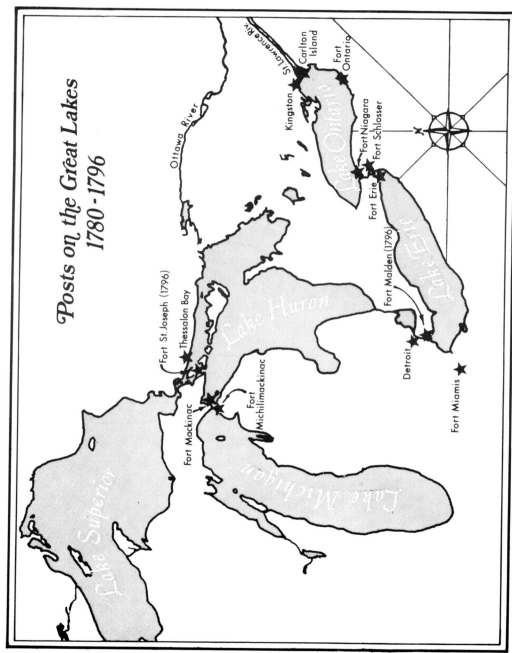

Posts on the Great Lakes 1780 - 1796

FIGURE 1.

later the Spanish on the Mississippi River. After the war, the main emphasis was on the protection of the fur trade and the control of the Indians.

The Great Lakes area was administered as part of Canada which was in itself administered separately from the rest of North America. The government of Canada was in the hands of the "Governor and Commander-in-Chief," stationed at Quebec. From 1778 to 1784, this post was held by General Frederick Haldimand, a Swiss in the service of Britain. General Guy Carleton (Lord Dorchester) held the post from 1786 until 1796, the same year in which the Americans finally occupied Fort Mackinac. Under the Governor there were military districts, commanded by the senior officer stationed in each. In 1793, there were four districts:[1]

1. Quebec — Three Rivers
2. Montreal
3. Kingston and dependencies (Carleton Island and Oswegatchie)
4. Upper Posts (Oswego, Niagara, Detroit and Mackinac)

In addition to the military commanders, there were also the Lieutenant Governors of Detroit and Michilimackinac whose positions were provided for by the Quebec Act of 1774. The status of these officials was somewhat vague and was the cause of much misunderstanding and ill feeling, as will be seen. The Lieutenant Governors were originally vested with civil powers, but, as these officials were former military men and held the principal responsibility for their posts, they felt that the military command of the post should also be theirs. After the departure of Lieutenant Governor Patrick Sinclair from Mackinac in 1782, however, there was never again a Lieutenant Governor stationed at Mackinac and the post was commanded by the senior military officer who was responsible to his regimental superior.

The Upper Posts of the Great Lakes were usually garrisoned by one or two regiments of Foot (Infantry). During the years of the American Revolution, however, the garrison of the area was somewhat larger. Mackinac was normally garrisoned by two companies of the regiment doing duty at the Upper Posts. This was increased during the Revolution to three companies and, from 1784 to 1786 and 1788-1789 reduced to only one company. The complement of these companies was nearly always under strength in both officers and men, and often two companies together equaled only a little more than a regulation company.

The Regiments of Foot in the British Army at the beginning of the American Revolution were divided between the English and the Irish Establishments. A regiment on the English Establishment was authorized to number 477 men and those on the Irish Establishment 474 men.[2] The terms regiment and battalion were virtually synonymous at the time and only two regiments that served at Mackinac had more than one battalion (the 60th and the 84th). A battalion of a regiment of more than one battalion would be referred to as "1st Battalion," or "2nd Battalion" etc. Thus, a unit would be known, for example, as the 1st Battalion, 84th Regiment of Foot (hereafter denoted as 1st/84th Foot). A regiment was nominally commanded by a Colonel, but was commanded in the field by its Lieutenant Colonel. Battalions were divided into ten companies, eight of which were known as "Battalion Companies," one as the "Grenadier Company," and one as the "Light Infantry Company." Grenadiers and Light Infantry were elite troops of the regiment. The Grenadiers were the largest and most impressive men and the Light n-fantry were active, specially trained skirmishers. Most of the Infantry companies that served at Fort Mackinac were Battalion Companies. An exception was the Grenadier Company of the 8th Foot which left the Straits of Mackinac in September of 1780. It is also possible that one of the two companies of the 2/60th Foot, in garrison from 1789 to 1790, was the Light Infantry Company.

Each infantry company was commanded by a Captain. Under him were a Lieutenant and an Ensign (Second Lieutenant). Two sergeants, three corporals and a drummer comprised the non-commissioned officers although, during the war of the Revolution, they were increased by one sergeant and one drummer. In 1775, a company on the English Establishment included 38 privates.[3] Early in the American Revolution this was raised to 56 privates[4] and, by 1781, it seems to have been 71 privates.[5] With the end of the American Revolution, the number of men in the British Army was drastically reduced and the authorized number of privates shrank first to 51 and then to 45 men. Units on active service were always under strength, however. Deaths, desertions, sickness, men sent off on special duty and the lack of replacements usually kept the size of companies below their established strength.

The clothing of British soldiers throughout the period 1780-1796 was dictated by the Warrant of 1768 which set down standard clothing rules for the British Army. In general, a British infantryman of the late eighteenth century wore a long, dull red, double-breasted coat, the lapels of which were buttoned back to show the facings so that the coat hung open in the front. Different regiments were distinguished by the color of their lapels, cuffs, and collars. The Warrant of 1768 established facing colors for the seventy regiments of Foot then in existence. They included various shades of yellow, red, green, buff, white, black

FIGURE 2. Private, 34th Foot.

and orange. Blue was reserved for "Royal" regiments. The units were further distinguished by the regimental lace which was of a white worsted material with stripes of different colors running through it. This lace was used to trim the mens' buttonholes on the lapels, cuffs, and collar and was usually applied in a rectangular shape. Some regiments, however, wore lace of a "bastion" shape (pointed at one end and the sides) and some regiments also had the buttons on the men's lapels arranged in pairs. The pewter buttons of the enlisted men were inscribed with the regimental number and some of these buttons have been found at Fort Mackinac. The overall effect was to enable a knowledgeable person to recognize the different units at a distance.

The linings of the men's coats were white (except for buff-faced units; theirs were buff) and thus the turnbacks, where the corners of the coattails were hooked up, were also of that color. Waistcoats and breeches were white (except for buff-faced units which had buff) and black linen gaiters were worn over the stockings. These gaiters were over the knee but, for the sake of comfort and freedom, short black gaiters were commonly worn.

The hats worn by the men were somewhat flatter versions of the earlier tri-corn hat, known as a "cocked hat." All three sides were turned up and the edges of the hat were trimmed in white tape. A black cockade was worn on the left side of the hat. In the later 1780s and 1790s these hats became even flatter until they nearly resembled bicorns and colored feathers were worn over the cockade. Also at that time the coat collars, which had previously been worn flat on the neck, began to be made to stand up. The white waistcoats were cut shorter and knee-length gaiters came into year around use.

Drummers usually wore a coat of the facing color of the unit, faced in red and trimmed in regimental lace. The exceptions were the blue-faced "Royal" regiments who wore red faced blue, trimmed in "Royal" lace and red-faced regiments who wore white faced red. Drummers who wore buff or white coats also wore red waist-

FIGURE 3. Drummer, 47th Foot.

coats and breeches instead of white ones. Small black bearskin caps (similar to those worn by the Grenadiers) were worn by drummers and the fronts of their drums were painted the facing color of the regiment with the King's Cypher and crown and the regimental number below it.

Sergeants were dressed much the same as the private soldiers except that their coats were scarlet and of a slightly better quality. Their hats were trimmed in silver lace and they wore plain white lace around their buttonholes. Sergeants wore a

FIGURE 4. Sergeant, 53rd Foot.

crimson sash with a stripe of the regimental facing color in the middle. For red-faced regiments, the stripe was to be white.

The coats of the officers were also of scarlet and of a much better material than those of the men. Regiments were either "gold" or "silver" regiments, referring to the type of lace worn by the officers, and their buttons, epaulettes, lace and hat trim were of the material specified for their unit. Officers also wore plain crimson sashes and metal, half moon-shaped plates, called gorgets, hung from their necks. The King's Arms and the regimental number were engraved upon the gorget

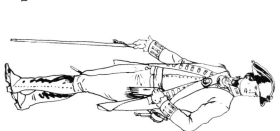

FIGURE 5. Officer, 65th Foot.

and they were either gold or silver, according to the color specified for the officers' lace. Officers of Battalion Companies wore an epaulette on the right shoulder; Grenadier and Light Infantry officers one on each shoulder.[6]

The men of the British Infantry were armed with a .75 calibre, smoothbore, flintlock musket known popularly as the "Brown Bess." The weapon was loaded from the muzzle with a prepared paper cartridge and it could be fired as often as four times a minute by a competent soldier. It was, however, extremely inaccurate and it was virtually impossible to hit a target at a range of over 100 yards. A good marksman, however, could usually hit a man-sized target at a range of 60 to 80 yards. The weapon weighed about 12 pounds and a long bayonet was carried for it.

By 1780, privates almost universally wore a pair of white leather cross belts supporting a cartridge box on the right side and a bayonet on the left side. Sergeants carried a sword and a halberd, but often discarded these for the more practical musket. Officers carried swords and espontoons.

Like the sergeant's halberd, the spear-like espontoon was also commonly discarded.

The life of a soldier was, at best, a hard one. Service was ordinarily for life[7] although, during the American Revolution, many men were enlisted for three years or the duration of the war and were discharged in 1783-84.[8] The life of an 18th century soldier was certainly not an easy one. The daily pay for a private of Foot was 8 pence of which the soldier probably saw very little, for most of his pay was withheld to pay for his food, uniform and numerous other "services."[9] What little pay was forthcoming was probably slow in reaching Mackinac and one complaint included in the petition of the men of two companies of the 8th Foot, drawn up in 1780, was that they had not received their back pay.[10]

Discipline was harsh in armies of the day, and punishments were brutal. In July, 1790, Sergeant Thomas Dunn of the 2nd/60th Foot was accused by some local traders of passing counterfeit currency to pay his bills. When ordered by his Commanding Officer, Captain John Parr, to wait in a room for the guard, Dunn disregarded the order and ran off. Although the charges of forgery were prominently brought out in the ensuing Court

FIGURE 6. Sergeant, 2nd/60th Foot.

Martial, the presiding officers were far more interested in the first charge: disrespect to the Commanding Officer and disorderly and unsoldierlike behaviour. For this infraction the sergeant was broken to the ranks, ordered to perform the duties of "private centinel" and sentenced to receive two hundred lashes. As was common, the flogging was to be administered by the drummers of the detachment. As to the charge of passing forged bills, the court did not "think itself competent to pass sentence on that matter."[11]

FIGURE 7. Soldiers' Barracks, Fort Michilimackinac. About seventy men lived in this wooden building.

The soldiers of the British Army were not physically large by modern standards, although men were not supposed to be enlisted if they stood under 5 feet 6½ inches tall.[12] Regulation food was monotonous and often bad or spoiled, and the only relief from it was food that the soldiers were able to grow or catch for themselves. In Canada, in 1779, seven rations consisted of:[13]

7 lbs. of Flour, of the first Quality, made from wholly Kiln-dried Wheat
7 lbs. of Beef, or in lieu thereof 4 lbs. of Pork
6 oz. of Butter or in lieu thereof 8 oz. of Cheese
3 pints of Pease
½ lb. of Oatmeal

Provision returns from Fort Mackinac show all of the first choice items except beef. Pork seems to have been a constant substitute,[14] and corn was often purchased by officers of the garrison, though it seems to have been for the use of the Indian Department. Rum was also a common commodity and very important in the daily life of the soldier. The daily ration was about a gill and a half (roughly 3/8 pint).[15] Beer seems not to have been carried on the storehouse inventory at Fort Mackinac.

For some soldiers life was made a little easier by the fact that it was possible for their wives to accompany them on active service. Soldiers also occasionally married local girls and several entries in the Ste. Anne parish register record these unions. In 1787 William Aiken, an Artillery-man, married Elizabeth McDonald, a daughter of a discharged sergeant of the 8th Foot and in 1781, George Paterson of the 8th Foot married off his daughter, Margaret, to Thomas Stone. Even officers occasionally succumbed to matrimony with a local girl as did Ensign Hamilton of the 5th Foot when he married Louisa Mitchell, daughter of former Surgeon's Mate David Mitchell, in 1791.[16]

Most soldiers, however, had to be content with barracks life. Although crowded together and plagued by ramshackle buildings and equipment, enlisted men did have a few small comforts. Their barracks at Mackinac were heated by wood-burning metal stoves, lit by candles and furnished with tables. They made up their beds with bed cases, bolster cases, sheets and blankets. The barracks were also furnished with numerous small rugs, obviously to make cold wooden floors somewhat more tolerable.[17]

FIGURE 8. Officers' Stone Barracks, Fort Mackinac, begun in 1781. Before its completion, many of the Fort's officers lived in the town.

Life for the officers was far removed from that of the men, although deductions were also made from officer's pay and junior officers were sometimes hard pressed to maintain their standard of living. Those officers who could afford it were allowed to live in rooms or houses rented from local merchants, and although the expense was no doubt greater, the added comfort and privacy must have been well worth it.[18] The pay for a Captain was 10 shillings a day, a Lieutenant 4 shillings 8 pence, and an Ensign 3 shillings 8 pence.[19] Officers, however, were often comfortably wealthy and their position at garrisons such as Fort Mackinac allowed the less honest ones an opportunity to increase what wealth they had, such as Captain Daniel Robertson seems to have done between 1782 and 1787.[20]

Most officers came from the wealthy English aristocracy and influence, patronage, and wealth played a major part in a man's advancement in rank. Families would often have several members in the same regiment and the family of Ensign John Bromhead, who served at Fort Mackinac in the 1790s, had been sending sons into the 24th Foot since 1756.[21] They continued to do so for at least another century and one member of the family, Lieutenant Gonville Bromhead ("B" Company, 2nd/24th Regiment of Foot), later won a Victoria Cross as second in command of the defense of Rorke's Drift during the Zulu War of 1879.[22]

Advancement was usually by purchase and Lieutenant Governor Patrick Sinclair purchased his commission as a Captain in the 1st/84th Foot in 1780. Sinclair probably did not have to pay top dollar for his commission, however, as the officer who was selling had to sell quickly because of poor health and the regiment was one that was likely to be disbanded at the end of hostilities. Had this not been the case, Sinclair might have paid as much as £1,500, which was the going rate for a Captaincy in 1776.[23]

One unfortunate result of the purchase system was that wealthy Englishmen were able to enter the service with relatively high rank regardless of whether they possessed any military experience. In 1790, Ensign George Forneret had the audacity to tell Captain John Parr, the commandant of Fort Mackinac and his superior officer, that he (Parr) ". . . cou'd known nothing of the Duty of a Captain" as he "had never mounted a guard as such since (he) had joined the 60th Regt. . ." and that since he "had not held the same rank in another Regt. (he) cou'd not have learnt it before." Despite the fact that Parr admitted to his lack of "professional knowledge" young Forneret was only spared a court martial because of the shortage of officers at Fort Mackinac and Parr's resulting inability to form a court.[24]

Despite the situation, however, the majority of British officers were honest, dedicated, soldiers, though jealous of their prerogatives and positions. The Great Lakes area was large and the system of command and supply much less than ideal, but the garrisons of Fort Mackinac functioned efficiently enough for sixteen years and helped the British control and regulate a prosperous and vital fur trade.

THE WAR YEARS 1780-1784

The British Army had maintained a garrisoned post at the Straits of Mackinac since 1761 when Fort Michilimackinac (at present-day Mackinaw City) was taken over from the French. Michilimackinac served as British military and administrative headquarters in the far northern Great Lakes and was usually garrisoned by one or two companies of regular infantry and a small detachment of the Royal Regiment of Artillery.

In 1774, two companies of the 8th or King's Regiment of Foot arrived at Fort Michilimackinac and these men formed the last garrison of that post and the first of Fort Mackinac. On 1 January 1780, the garrison numbered:[25]

3 Lieutenants
1 Surgeon's Mate
3 Sergeants
2 Drummers
66 Rank and File

These men were part of two under strength companies: the Grenadier Company and the "General's" Company.[26] They were under the command of Lieutenant George Clowes of the 8th, though the post itself was commanded by Lieutenant Governor Patrick Sinclair.

The 8th Foot had arrived at Quebec in 1768, and by the time this unit was stationed at Fort Michilimackinac, their uniforms were patterned on the Warrant of 1768. The coats of the men were faced with dark blue and the linings and turnbacks were white. The regimental lace was white with one blue and one yellow stripe. En-

FIGURE 9. Officer's and enlisted man's buttons of the 8th Foot.

listed mens' buttons were pewter, with "Ks8" on them. Officers had gold lace, buttons and epaulettes. The General's Company was a Battalion Company and wore regular cocked hats while the Grenadiers wore fur caps. Lieutenant Clowes was probably the only officer of the Grenadiers and he would have worn an epaulette on each shoulder.[27]

The garrison of Michilimackinac was already making preparations to move the post to Mackinac Island and, during the winter of 1779-1780, a small detachment of the 8th was clearing ground and preparing materials on the Island.[28] The move was intended to make the British position in the Straits more secure against a possible American attack, and was being directed by Patrick Sinclair, "Lieutenant Governor and Superintendant of Michilimackinac." Sinclair had arrived at the Straits on 4 October 1779,[29] and had replaced Major Arent S. DePeyster, of the 8th, as commandant.

Lieutenant Governor Sinclair was in a rather confusing predicament. He was a military man of twenty-five years' experience, but was presently without an active commission. His rank in the Army was Captain, but he was not given control of the troops of the garrison; they were to remain under the command of the senior officer of the 8th at the post.[30] Sinclair had complained to General Frederick Haldimand, the Governor of Canada, about this situation even before he embarked for

Michilimackinac. He felt very strongly that, while he was made responsible for the security of Michilimackinac, he had no control over the troops who maintained that security.[31] Although problems centering on the ambiguous situation of Lieutenant Governors had already arisen at Detroit, Haldimand had no solution to the problem until he received word from England, and he, therefore, had ordered Sinclair to Michilimackinac to take over his civil duties.[32]

Shortly thereafter, Haldimand came upon a possible solution to this problem. His idea was to obtain for Sinclair a commission in a unit stationed at Michilimackinac, which would give him both civil and military command of the post.[33] An opportunity to implement this finally appeared in the spring of 1780. Sinclair was allowed to purchase the Captaincy of Captain George McDougall, of the 1st/84th Regiment of Foot, who was in extremely poor health.[34] Sinclair's new commission was effective 1 April 1780.[35]

The next step was to station some men of Sinclair's new regiment at Michilimackinac. At this point Haldimand was able to solve two problems at once. Sinclair needed some men of his regiment to give substance to his claim to the military command of Michilimackinac and artificers (troops possessing construction skills) were badly needed to help build the new fort on Mackinac Island. The result was that one sergeant, one corporal and twelve privates of the 1st/84th were ordered to the Straits of Mackinac in April 1780.[36] Some of these men had been working with the Engineer's Department while others were to have been taken from Sinclair's (formerly McDougall's) Company. These men arrived at Michilimackinac early in June.[37] Nine more men were sent in September,[38] and Sinclair was given permission to recruit as many additional men as was necessary to complete a full company of the 1st/84th (73, later 56 men). The men were to be recruited for the duration of the ''American War.''[39]

The 84th Regiment of Foot had been raised in Canada in 1775 as the Royal Highland Emigrants.[40] Most of its recruits had come from former Highland soldiers who had settled in Canada at the end

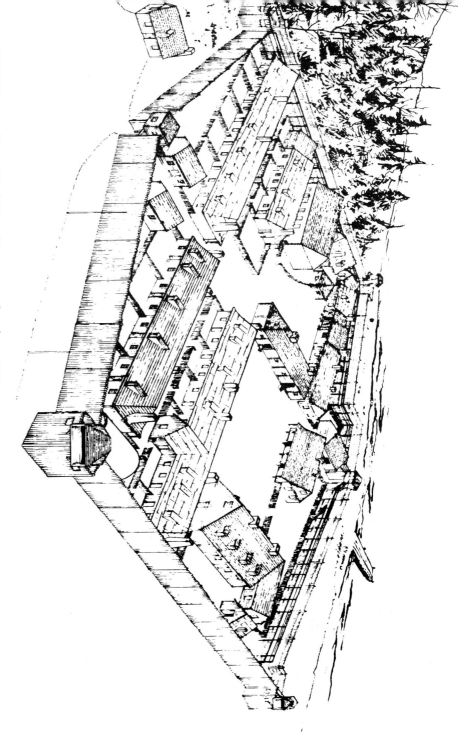

FIGURE 10. Fort Michilimackinac in the late 1770s.

of the Seven Years War. The regiment consisted of two battalions of ten companies each, and the men who served at Mackinac were of the 1st Battalion. In 1779, the *Royal Highland Emigrants* had been placed on the Regular Establishment and had been given the number "84."[41] Information concerning the uniform of this regiment is vague, but in 1775, they were to be uniformed "in like manner with His Majesty's Royal Highland Regiment (42nd Foot) . . ."[42] Kilts were worn by the 84th in the 1770s,[43] and when the detachment of this unit was sent to Michilimackinac in 1780, this article of clothing was probably still in use, although trousers were also possibly worn.[44] Old clothing was to be used for fatigue duty and since the men stationed at the Straits were artificers, they no doubt spent much of their time in working clothes.[45] Blanket coats and fur caps were worn during the winter months and this seems to have been the case with most British troops in Canada at this period.[46]

A private of the 84th at Mackinac, dressed for doing regular duty, quite probably wore a Highland bonnet with a cockade and, perhaps, a feather. The red coat would have been faced blue with white lace containing one red, one blue and one red stripe.[47] The lace for officers was gold. Enlisted mens' buttons were pewter with a wreath, thistle and the number "84."[48] The waistcoat was white and the waistbelt was black leather with a cartridge box and bayonet frog attached. Plaids and kilts were worn,[49] but trousers and even trews are also mentioned.[50] In 1782, the men were issued both shoes and mocassins.[51]

During the summer of 1780 there was another change in the composition of the garrison of Fort

Michilimackinac. The men of the two companies of the *8th* sent a petition to Major DePeyster in Detroit.[52] The petition was directed against Lieutenant Clowes and centered mostly upon poor conditions and delays in pay.[53] A relatively minor point was that Clowes insisted that the soldiers appear ". . . as clean for duty as when we lay at Quebec dressed everyway the same and powdered. . ,"[54] a definite difficulty on the frontier, but apparently the men at Michilimackinac powdered their hair and kept their uniforms as close to regulation as possible.

By sending the petition to DePeyster, the troops went over the head of both Clowes and Sinclair, who was now their rightful superior, and this resulted in further ill feeling. The Grenadier Company had been the most voluble in complaining and, in August, 1780, it was relieved by Captain John Mompesson's Battalion Company. Mompesson and part of his company arrived 21 August[55] and the exchange was completed sometime in September.

The winter of 1780-81 found a somewhat larger garrison at the Straits of Mackinac than that of the previous winter:[56]

8th Foot
1 Captain
1 Lieutenant
1 Ensign
1 Surgeon's Mate
4 Sergeants
2 Drummers
75 Rank and Rile

1st/84th Foot
1 Lieutenant Governor (Captain)
1 Sergeant
22 Rank and File

Royal Artillery
1 Corporal
1 Matross

Unfortunately, the replacement of the Grenadier Company and some of the officers who did not get along with Sinclair did not bring peace to the garrison of Fort Michilimackinac. As soon as Captain Mompesson arrived at Michilimackinac, he began disputing Sinclair's right to command the military detachment. Mompesson felt that he should be senior to Sinclair in this matter because of the latter's long period without an active commission.[57] The question of Sinclair's position was finally settled in September 1780, by General Haldimand who confirmed Sinclair's right to overall command at the Straits of Mackinac.[58] The ill feeling persisted, however, and Sinclair was never able to get along well with the officers and men of the 8th.

FIGURE 11. Grenadier private, 8th Foot.

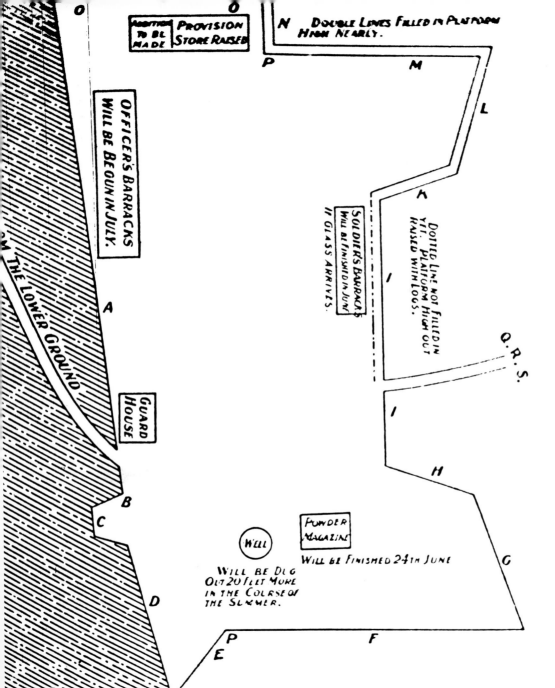

FIGURE 13. Lieutenant Governor Sinclair's plan of the new Fort on Mackinac Island, 1781.

The diagram includes the following labels:

- O O
- ADDITION TO BE MADE | PROVISION STORE RAISED
- N DOUBLE LINES FILLED IN PLATFORM HIGH NEARLY.
- OFFICER'S BARRACKS WILL BE BEGUN IN JULY.
- THE LOWER GROUND
- SOLDIER'S BARRACKS WILL BE FINISHED IN JUNE IF GLASS ARRIVES.
- DOTTED LINE NOT FILLED IN YET. PLATFORM HIGH OUT RAISED WITH LOGS.
- Q. R. S.
- GUARD HOUSE
- WELL — WILL BE DUG OUT 20 FEET MORE IN THE COURSE OF THE SUMMER.
- POWDER MAGAZINE — WILL BE FINISHED 24TH JUNE
- P M L K I I H G F E P D C B A

FIGURE 12. Officer, 8th Foot.

Work, meanwhile, continued on the new fort on Mackinac Island and Captain Mompesson spent the winter there, directing the construction. The final move from the mainland to Mackinac Island was made during 1781 and half of the garrison had been transferred by July.[59] As early as April, Captain Mompesson had been drilling the troops in the defense of the new fort, but attempted never to keep them under arms for more than an hour ". . . on account of their gardens."[60]

The tensions between Captain Sinclair and the men of the 8th never really subsided, however, and in June, 1781 General Haldimand ordered the two companies of the 8th Foot to be replaced by an equal number of the 47th Foot. Only Surgeon's Mate David Mitchell and Sergeant Phillips of the 8th were to remain.[61] Captain Thomas Aubrey, who was to command the detachment of the 47th, was reminded of the harmony that was necessary for the smooth operation of a military post.[62] Despite this advice, however, Aubrey sent a memorial to General Haldimand expressing his displeasure at having to replace Mompesson and the 8th because of the tensions in the command situation at Mackinac.[63] This was apparently to no avail and Captain Aubrey, Lieutenant Ford and about fifty men of the 47th Foot arrived at Mackinac Island on 8 August.[64] Mompesson and some of his men left on 20 August [65] and the relief was completed on 13 September with the arrival of Ensign Hamilton and the remainder of the detachment of the 47th.[66]

The headquarters of the 47th Regiment was established at Fort Mackinac because Captain Aubrey was commanding what remained of the regiment. Most of the regiment had been surrendered to the Americans at Saratoga in 1777 and only about two and a half companies remained in service in Canada. The detachment for Mackinac was drawn about equally from Captain Aubrey's and Captain Gamble's Companies, plus the partial company. The remainder of these companies was stationed at Detroit.[67]

The uniforms of the men of the 47th Foot were faced with white and their lace was white with one red and two black stripes. Their pewter but-

8th Foot
1 Surgeon's Mate
1 Sergeant

1st/84th Foot
1 Lieutenant Governor (Captain)
1 Sergeant
34 Rank and File

Royal Artillery
1 Corporal
1 Matross

The 47th Foot made up the bulk of the Fort Mackinac garrison until August, 1782 when the decision was made to draft the rank and file of the 47th into the 8th. The officers, sergeants, and drummers of the former unit were replaced by those of the 8th and sent home to England to recruit new companies.[70] Lieutenant Clowes, Ensigns Fry and Pollard, four sergeants and two drummers of the 8th Foot arrived in September to take over the rank and file of the 47th.[71] As of 25 October 1782, the rank and file of the 47th Foot officially became part of the 8th,[72] though they probably continued to wear their white-faced coats for awhile until blue-faced coats of the 8th became available.

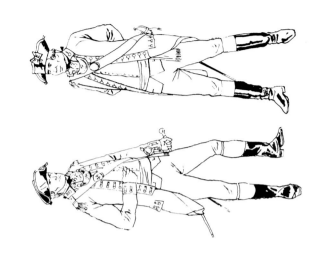

FIGURE 15. Field Officer, 44th Foot; Officer, Corps of Engineers.

FIGURE 14. Enlisted man's pewter button, 47th Foot.

tons had a "47" within a scalloped border. The officers' lace, buttons and epaulettes were silver, but lace was not applied around their buttonholes.[68] Otherwise, their uniform was virtually identical to that of the 8th.

In January, 1782 Fort Mackinac had its largest garrison of the period 1780-1796:[69]

47th Foot
1 Captain
2 Lieutenants
4 Sergeants
2 Drummers
73 Rank and File

The 47th Foot left Fort Mackinac in the fall of 1782, and so did Patrick Sinclair, the new fort's first commandant. On 18 September 1782 Sinclair was replaced by Captain Daniel Robertson,[73] also of the 1st/84th and previously assigned to Oswegatchie on the St. Lawrence River. Sinclair had incurred large expenses in the construction of the new fort and, despite his promises, it was still far from being completed in September 1782. An inspection partly comprised of Sir John Johnson, James Stanley Goddard, Lieutenant Colonel Henry Hope of the 44th Foot and Lieutenant Richard Hockings of the *Corps of Engineers*[74] arrived in that month to find that the fort was not even in a defensible shape against Indians, and that the present garrison was inadequate to hold the rambling works. Hockings was the first real engineer to see Fort Mackinac, and although he was not pleased with it, he thought that 100 laborers would be able to put the fort in a defensible shape within two months.[75] Captain Robertson, nevertheless, assumed command with strict instructions to cut down on expenses at the post.[76]

The Fort Mackinac garrison of January, 1783 was somewhat reduced in numbers from that of 1782:[77]

8th Foot
1 Lieutenant
2 Ensigns
1 Surgeon's Mate
3 Sergeants
2 Drummers
65 Rank and File

1st/84th Foot
1 Captain
1 Ensign
32 Rank and File

Royal Artillery
1 Corporal
1 Matross

FIGURE 16. Officer's button, 55th Foot.

The year 1783 brought the end of the War of the American Revolution, but also was the beginning of new problems for the commandant of Fort Mackinac. The fort was included in the area ceded by Great Britian to the United States by the Treaty of Paris. The British thereafter were concerned about their continuing control of the fur trade and the Indians of the Upper Great Lakes and, although the war had officially ended, the garrison of Fort Mackinac remained at about 100 men until the summer of 1784. The possibility that the British garrison would have to evacuate the post for the other side of the new boundary was recognized by Captain Robertson who suggested in July, 1783 that Tessalon Bay (in present-day Ontario) be selected as the site of the new post when

the move became necessary. Tessalon Bay is about seventy-five miles northeast of Mackinac and is fairly close to the mouth of the St. Mary's River. Robertson felt that the Great Lakes Indians could still be effectively controlled from there. A few men seem to have been sent to Tessalon on Robertson's own initiative,[79] but little, if anything, was done in 1783.

Occasionally individual soldiers would be sent off on special duty to posts that were not garrisoned by their regiment and, in the summer of 1783, this was the case at Fort Mackinac. Between the months of April and July, 1783 the returns of the *1st Battalion, King's Royal Regiment of New York* show a sergeant of that unit on detached duty to Fort Mackinac.[80] What this duty was is unclear, but the request for the services of this man was made to Brigadier General von Specht at Montreal in October, 1782. The request was for a man who had been on that duty before[81] and he was probably a courier of some sort.

The *King's Royal Regiment of New York* was an American Loyalist unit that had been raised by Sir John Johnson (son of Sir William Johnson) in Western New York at the beginning of the American Revolution. The individuals of this unit who went on this special duty to Fort Mackinac were the only Loyalist troops to serve there during the Revolution. By 1783, the *King's Royal Regiment of New York* wore uniforms like those of the regulars and their red coats were faced in dark blue. A sergeant of the unit would have worn plain white lace around his buttonholes, which were possibly arranged in pairs. An existing portrait of an officer of the regiment and an original officer's coat have the lace arranged in pairs, but this does not necessarily mean that the lace of the non-commissioned officers and men was similarly arranged.[82] Enclosed within a wreath on the pewter buttons of this unit was "K-R NEW YORK."[83]

Individuals of other regiments might have served at Fort Mackinac as couriers, transfers and replacements. An officer's button of the 55th Foot, for example, has been found at the fort although this regiment was not even serving in Canada at the time of the American Revolution. Another button discovery was a pewter enlisted man's button of the 44th Foot, possibly dropped by a servant of Lt. Col. Hope during his inspection tour in 1782.

By the beginning of 1784, the garrison was still roughly at the strength it had been for several years:

8th Foot [84]
1 Lieutenant
1 Ensign
1 Surgeon's Mate
3 Sergeants
2 Drummers
62 Rank and File

1st/84th Foot [85]
1 Officer
34 Rank and File

Royal Artillery
not included in this return.

As of the spring of 1784, Captain Robertson had not yet received any instructions regarding the fate of his post. In May, however, General Haldimand sent Captain Robertson orders to look over possible sites for a new post, but not to begin any work until receiving further orders. A place referred to as Point Aux Pins had been suggested to Haldimand, but Robertson was to take a look for himself, paying particular attention that the site was within the British side of the treaty line,

was as close to Mackinac as possible, was convenient to the entrance to Lake Superior and offered a safe harbor for sailing vessels. [86] Robertson made his inspection tour during the first week of June and once again suggested Tessalon Bay to Haldimand. [87] He also sent a non-commissioned officer and twelve men to ". . . clear a little ground by way of amusement." [88] In August, however, Robertson was informed that the surrender of the Great Lakes posts was not imminent and that no further work was to be done at Tessalon. [89]

The work at Tessalon came at about the same time that the reduction of Fort Mackinac's garrison was beginning. During the summer of 1784, the 1st/84th was disbanded and, in March, Robertson was ordered to send his men of this unit down the Lakes. [90] Captain Robertson was himself a member of the 1st/84th, but he was to remain at Fort Mackinac as civil and military commander. [91] Robertson objected to sending down the men of the 84th, mainly because his best artificers were men of this unit, and he felt that the work at Tessalon could not be carried on without them. [92] The men were sent down late in June, [93] however, and the work at Tessalon ceased shortly thereafter.

The 8th Foot was also being reduced, though not disbanded, during the summer of 1784. Many of the men in this regiment had been enlisted only for the duration of the war and the reductions were completed in June. [94] By July, Fort Mackinac was garrisoned only by men of the 8th and a few men of the Royal Regiment of Artillery. The detachment of the 8th Foot was very small: [95]

1 Lieutenant
1 Ensign
1 Surgeon's Mate
2 Sergeants
1 Drummer
34 Rank and File

The long tenure of the 8th Foot at the Straits of Mackinac was also about to end and, on 4 August 1784, the remaining men of that unit were relieved by a small detachment of the 34th Foot. [96] The 8th was much in need of relief, for they had been on duty in canada for seventeen years and, a year later, in 1785, they were described as being more a ". . . regiment of invalids than soldiers." [97] Even when they finally did leave for England, in 1785, some of the men were drafted into the 53rd Foot, which was later to serve at Fort Mackinac. [98]

The first four years of Fort Mackinac's existence had coincided with the last years of the American Revolution. Mackinac had been important as a trading post and as a base by which to control

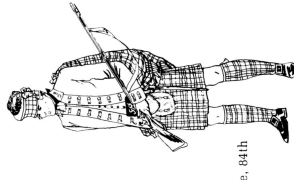

FIGURE 17. Private, 84th Foot.

1. Private, Grenadier Company, 8th or King's Regiment of Foot, 1780.

2. Officer, Battalion Company, 8th or King's Regiment of Foot, 1780-1784.

3. Private, Royal Regiment of Artillery, 1780.

4. Private, 1st Battalion, 84th or Royal Highland Emigrant Regiment of Foot, 1780-1784.

DIRK GRINGHUIS

5. Drummer, 47th Regiment of Foot, 1781-1782.

6. Field Officer, 44th Regiment of Foot, 1782.

7. Officer, Corps of Engineers, 1782.

8. Private, Mackinac Militia, c. 1784.

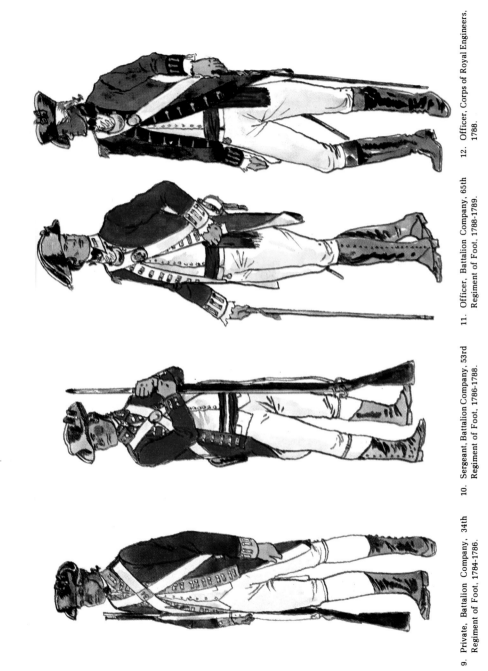

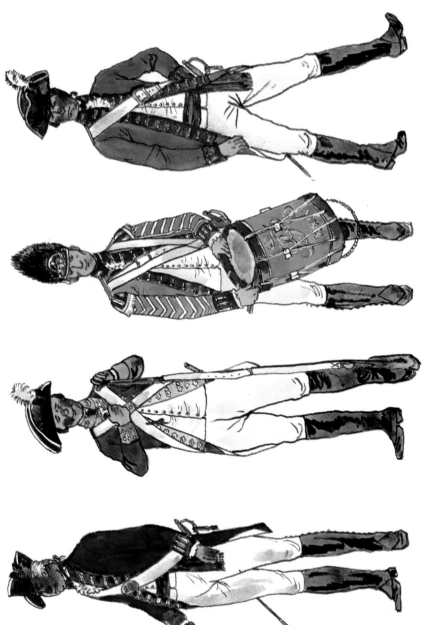

12. Officer, Corps of Royal Engineers, 1788.

11. Officer, Battalion Company, 65th Regiment of Foot, 1788-1789.

10. Sergeant, Battalion Company, 53rd Regiment of Foot, 1786-1788.

9. Private, Battalion Company, 34th Regiment of Foot, 1784-1786.

16. Sergeant, Royal Regiment of Artillery, 1796.

15. Drummer, 24th Regiment of Foot, 1792-1796.

14. Private, Battalion Company, 5th Regiment of Foot, 1790-1792.

13. Sergeant, Battalion Company, 2nd Battalion, 60th or Royal American Regiment of Foot, 1789-1790.

the Northern Great Lakes. With the conclusion of the war, Mackinac was as important as ever to the British, but its future was very much in doubt. No further work was to be done on the fortifications because of the possibility of an American takeover and, because of the wholesale Army reductions, the garrison was very small by the end of 1784. From 1784 until 1796, it was expected that the post might have to be given up at any time, and decisions concerning Fort Mackinac were always to be colored by this fact.

THE LATE 1780s
1784-1790

The garrison that relieved the 8th Foot in August, 1784 was one of the smallest ever to have served at Fort Mackinac. Ensign George Dodsworth brought with him to Fort Mackinac only one sergeant, one drummer and twenty-five rank and file.[99] Captain Daniel Robertson, formerly of the 1st/84th, and now without a regiment, still commanded the Fort.

The 34th Foot had arrived in America in 1775,[100] and had spent most of the War of the American Revolution in Lower Canada, near Lake Champlain and the St. Lawrence River. They were a yellow-faced regiment and their white lace had a blue and yellow worm and a red stripe running through it. Their buttonholes were arranged in pairs,[101] and the pewter buttons of the enlisted men were marked "34." The lace, epaulettes and buttons of

FIGURE 18. Officer's button, 34th.

the officers were silver, and a fine officer's button has been found at Fort Mackinac. The pattern of the uniform was still based on the Warrant of 1768.[102]

Despite the weakness of the garrison, Head Quarters in Quebec was not worried about Fort Mackinac because of the cessation of work on the fort and the assistance that could be derived from the Indians for its defense.[103] By May, 1785, in fact, there were only twenty rank and file of the

34th in the garrison.[104] The garrison was finally increased to a more practical number in June, 1785:

34th Foot[105]
  1 Ensign
  2 Sergeants
  48 Rank and File
Royal Artillery[106]
  1 Non-commissioned Officer
  2 Gunners

In July, Ensign Dodsworth was replaced by Ensign Alexander McDonald as the officer of the 34th in the garrison.[107] From September, 1785 to May, 1786 the garrison is listed simply as "one company" of the 34th Foot.[108]

In August, 1786 the 34th was relieved by the 53rd Foot, another regiment that had been in Canada since the American Revolution. It had arrived at Quebec 1 June 1776,[109] and had served in Lower Canada until it was sent up the Lakes. Lieutenant Thomas Hughes of the regiment was stationed in Detroit from 1786 until 1788 and his journal gives an entertaining, if somewhat brief, description of his travels and duties in the Great Lakes.[110]

Hughes records, in August, 1786, that Lieutenant Houghton and a detachment of forty men of the 53rd were detached to Mackinac to relieve "... the troops at present there." [111] "The 34th then proceeded down the Lakes and returned to Europe in 1787." [112]

The men of Fort Mackinac's new garrison wore dull red coats with collars, lapels, and cuffs of the same color. The mens' pewter buttons were stamped with a "53." [113] and were arranged singly on their coats. The lace was white with a single red stripe. The facings of the officers were scarlet to go with their scarlet coats and their lace, epaulettes and buttons were gold. The uniform of the 53rd Foot was cut in the same style as it had been during the American Revolution.[114]

At the end of 1786, Captain Daniel Robertson was still commanding the Post of Mackinac and his garrison consisted of: [115]

53rd Foot
  1 Lieutenant
  1 Ensign
  1 Sergeant
  42 Rank and File
Royal Artillery
  6 Rank and File "doing duty"
  1 Rank and File "in charge of ordnance stores"

Daniel Robertson continued as commander of Fort Mackinac until sometime in May or June of 1787. The reasons for his relief are obscure, but Robertson was apparently dabbling in the fur trade on his own and, reportedly, "made a for-tune."[116] A popular piece of Mackinac Island folklore connected with a cliff known as "Robin-son's Folly" (a corruption of Robertson) maintains that the Captain met his death on the cliff during a struggle with an Indian warrior over Robertson's Indian mistress.[117] A less romantic version has it that it was hallucinations or intoxication which caused the officer's fall from the cliff. Despite these stories, Captain Robertson seems to have survived his stay at Mackinac Island and he re-ceived half-pay as a retired Captain of the 1st/84th Foot until 1794.[118]

Robertson's successor was Captain Thomas Scott of the 53rd Foot, who arrived at Mackinac on 15 June 1787.[119] Among Scott's officers was Lieu-tenant Daniel Robertson, a nephew of Fort Macki-nac's former commander.[120] Scott also brought along a small reinforcement for the garrison and, in November, 1787 Fort Mackinac was held by:[121]

53rd Foot
1 Captain
2 Lieutenants
1 Ensign
2 Sergeants
1 Drummer
52 Rank and File

Royal Artillery
2 Rank and File "on duty"
1 Rank and File "in charge of stores"

Captain Scott was apparently much more discreet in respect to his personal interests than was Cap-tain Robertson for, when he left for England in the fall of 1788, he was very highly recommended to General Haldimand (then in England) for his honest handling of affairs at Mackinac.[122]

The 53rd remained at Fort Mackinac until the beginning of July, 1788. At that time, one of the five companies of the 65th Foot, which had ar-

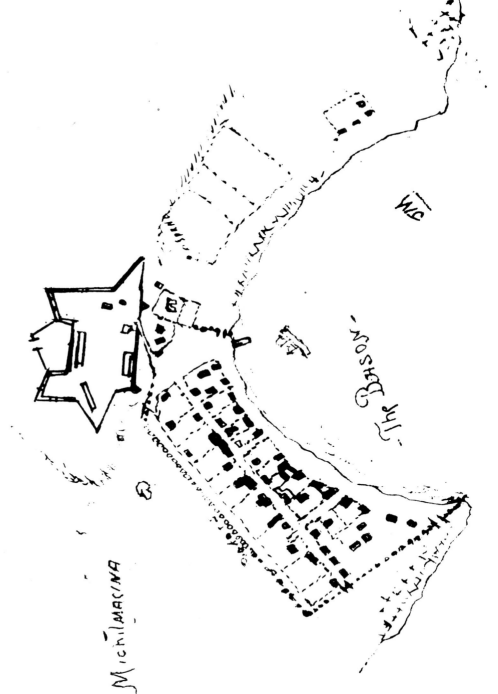

FIGURE 19. Fort Mackinac and the fortified town, 1780s.

rived to relieve the 53rd at Detroit, was sent to garrison Fort Mackinac.[123] The 65th was the first unit to serve at Mackinac that had not served in Canada during the War of the American Revolution. When they arrived at Mackinac in July, 1785, Lieutenant Hughes of the 53rd found them to be "so completely germanised in both dress and manoeuvres that it was some time before we could think them our brother soldiers . . . ."[124] This "germanisation" of dress probably refers to the minor changes in British uniform styles that were taking place during the last years of the 1780s. The cocked hats of the men became flatter and plumes were often worn in them. The collars of the coats were made to stand up, reaching just below the ears. Some or all of these changes were probably embodied by the 65th Foot, which was a white-faced regiment. The regimental lace contained a red and black worm and a black stripe. The lace for officers was silver and the buttons were marked '65.'[125]

The 65th Foot garrisoned Fort Mackinac until about June 1789 when they were relieved by troops of the 2nd Battalion, 60th Foot, under Captain John Parr. Information on the 65th at Mackinac is very scarce, other than that during this time the post was commanded by Captain Alexander Malcolm.[126]

There is also relatively little information about the 2nd/60th when they were in garrison at Fort Mackinac. The unit had arrived in Canada from the West Indies in 1787,[127] and the detachment that served at Mackinac was probably made up of two companies: one battalion company and possibly the Light Infantry Company, although both were doubtless under strength. The 60th Foot was no stranger to the Straits of Mackinac. The 1st Battalion had served at Fort Michilimackinac from 1761 to 1763 and the 2nd/60th from 1766 to 1772.[128] During the War of the American Revolution, they served in the West Indies and in the South, notably at Savannah, Georgia.[129]

The uniform of the 2nd/60th at this time probably had also incorporated the standing collar and the larger, flatter hat. The 60th Foot was known as the "Royal American Regiment" and, as a Royal regiment, wore dark blue facings on their uniforms. The evenly-spaced buttonholes of the enlisted men were trimmed in white lace containing two blue stripes. The mens' buttons were pewter with a "60" within a wreath. Lace for the officers was silver.[130]

The 2nd/60th remained at Fort Mackinac for little more than a year, and they saw the end of the 1780s at the Straits of Mackinac. When they were replaced by the 5th Foot, in the late summer of 1790, Fort Mackinac had technically been the property of the United States for seven years,

Little or no work had been done on the fort during that time other than necessary maintenance. The last officer of the Corps of Royal Engineers to inspect the post had been Captain Gother Mann, in 1788, and he found the place to be in poor repair, too large to defend properly and exposed to attack from the heights to the north.[131] Even so, by 1790 an American takeover of Fort Mackinac did not yet seem imminent.

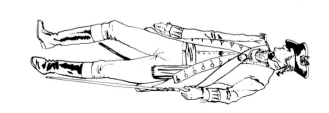

FIGURE 20. Officer, Corps of Royal Engineers, 1788.

THE 1790s
1790-1796

Late in the summer of 1790, two companies of the 5th Foot replaced the detachment of the 2nd/60th then in garrison.[132] They were under the command of Captain Edward Charlton who assumed the responsibility for the post of Mackinac. The 5th had been in Canada since 1787,[133] but this was their first duty in the far frontier posts. The uniforms of the 5th Foot included all of the alterations of the late 1780s, and a contemporary drawing from 1789 illustrates these changes.[134] The facings of this unit were "gosling green," a very dull shade of green, and the shape of the lace around the mens' buttonholes was of a type referred to as "bastion-shaped." The lace contained two red stripes and the pewter buttons were marked with the Roman Numeral "V". The lace for the officers was silver. The hats of the enlisted men each had a white plume stuck in them and the waistcoats were cut very square and short at the bottom.

Early in the 1790s, the United States finally began making moves against the Indians of the Northwest Territory, for the purpose of establishing American control over this area, which had

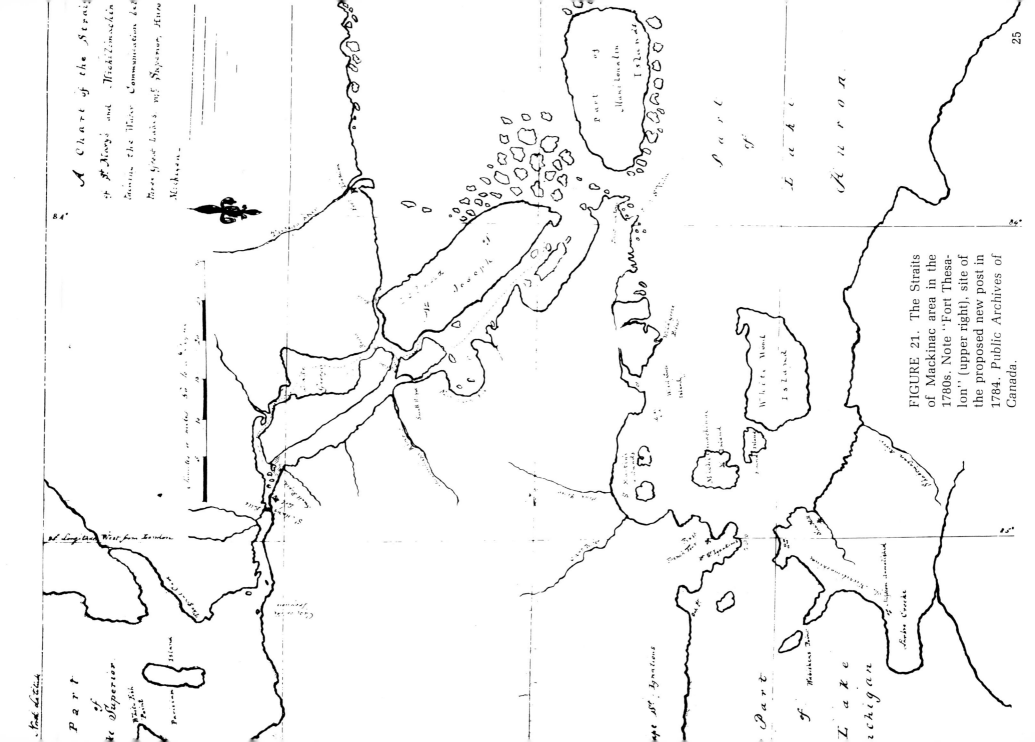

FIGURE 21. The Straits of Mackinac area in the 1780s. Note "Fort Thesalon" (upper right), site of the proposed new post in 1784. *Public Archives of Canada.*

been officially given up by the British in 1783. Despite the fact that American troops under Generals Harmar and St. Clair met disastrous setbacks at the hands of the Great Lakes Indians, the possibility of the Americans finally occupying the Great Lakes Posts became real. In 1794, General Anthony Wayne's victory at Fallen Timbers in Ohio, and James Jay's Treaty, signed in London, decided the fate of Fort Mackinac. An American takeover was only a matter of time.

When Captain Charlton and his companies of the 5th were replaced by Captain William Doyle and the 24th Foot on 1 July 1792, the last of the eighteenth century British garrisons arrived at the Straits of Mackinac. Doyle's garrison was fairly strong, especially in artilleryman, reflecting the increasing tensions on the Great Lakes Frontier. On 25 September 1792 the garrison of Fort Mackinac numbered: [135]

24th Foot
1 Captain
1 Lieutenant
1 Ensign
1 Surgeon's Mate
2 Sergeants
1 Drummer
54 Rank and File

Royal Artillery
1 Sergeant
1 Bombardier
7 Gunners

FIGURE 22. Enlisted man's button, 5th Foot.

As was the case with the 5th Foot, the facings of the 24th were green, though a darker, bluish shade known as "willow green." The white lace of the men was decorated with one green and one red stripe and the very plain pewter buttons were stamped "24". The plumes for the mens' hats were probably white over red and the lace and

FIGURE 24. Officer's and enlisted man's buttons, 24th Foot.

buttons of the officers were silver. [136]

The size of the Mackinac garrison remained nearly constant for the next two years and the last complete garrison return we have for the 1780-1796 period is dated 7 August 1795 and shows: [137]

24th Foot
1 Captain
2 Lieutenants
1 Ensign
1 Surgeon's Mate
2 Sergeants
1 Drummer
57 Rank and File

Royal Artillery
1 Sergeant
7 Rank and File

The Captain of the 24th listed above was still William Doyle, who continued as commander of

FIGURE 23. Private, 5th Foot.

Fort Mackinac. On 6 May 1795 he had been promoted Brevet Major in the Army [138] (though he still remained a Captain in the 24th) and his later correspondence from Mackinac is signed "Major William Doyle."

In 1796 the end came for the British garrisons of Fort Mackinac. The posts on the American side of the Great Lakes were to be given up and, on 4 April 1796, orders for the dispositions of the troops in Canada were issued. The 24th was to return to Lower Canada. [139] On 1 June, orders were given for the evacuation of the posts, and the entire garrison of Fort Mackinac, with the exception of a caretaker detachment of one Officer and twenty men, was to leave the place "with all convenient speed." [140]

In order to keep a garrison in the Northern Great Lakes, the British decided to fortify St. Joseph's Island, and in June, 1796 Lieutenant Andrew Foster and fourteen men began building temporary huts there. [141] Foster and his men of the 24th were replaced, probably in July, by Ensign Brown and fourteen men of the Queen's Rangers who were to comprise the garrison of St.

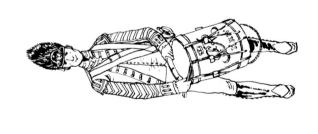

FIGURE 25. Drummer, 24th Foot.

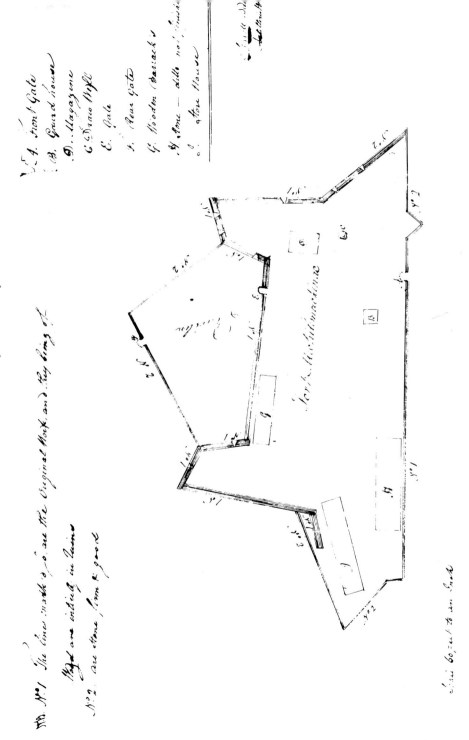

FIGURE 26. Fort Mackinac in 1796. *Historical Society of Pennsylvania.*

Joseph's Island.[142] Both Major Doyle and Thomas Duggan (Storekeeper of the Indian Department at Mackinac) expressed concern over the small size of this garrison in view of the future proximity of the Americans and the unfavorable impression of such a small force would make among the Indians.[143] Finally, late in September, St. Joseph's Island was garrisoned by one Captain and forty men of the Royal Canadian Volunteers. St. Joseph's Island and Fort St. Joseph were to be the British base in the Northern Great Lakes until the outbreak of the War of 1812, when Mackinac was recaptured and once again occupied by the British Army.

BRITISH ARTILLERY AT FORT MACKINAC 1780-1796

Artillery was an important part of the defenses of an eighteenth century military post and the guns of Fort Mackinac served a variety of purposes during the British occupation. They were fired as salutes on important occasions, they marked the beginning and end of each day and they were used to awe the Indians, who could never hope to control such monstrous weapons. By far their most important purpose, however, was to defend the walls of the fort and the town below.

The artillery at Fort Mackinac was made up of several types of weapons: guns (made of both brass and iron), howitzers (of iron), mortars (of brass) and wall pieces.

Guns were the standard cannon of the day and these weapons were designed to fire solid iron

Major Doyle was in Malden (Amherstburg, Ontario) in mid-August and the British vessels on the Lake were shuttling back and forth to remove most of the Mackinac garrison.[144] Although there is little information on the last days of Fort Mackinac as a British outpost, it was Lieutenant Foster who remained with a small detachment to await the arrival of the Americans.[145] The British expected to give up the fort to the Americans earlier in the summer, but a lack of provisions slowed down the occupying force.[146] Finally, on 1 September 1796, Major Henry Burbeck took over Fort Mackinac for the United States of America. Exactly what ceremonies, if any, took place are not recorded, but it was Lieutenant Foster's duty to inspect the installation with Major Burbeck and present that officer with a statement in writing, of the condition of the post. Major Burbeck signed a duplicate of the statement which Lieutenant Foster kept and delivered to the Adjutant General in Quebec.[147] When these few formalities were concluded, Lieutenant Foster and his men embarked for Lower Canada and left Fort Mackinac in the hands of its first American garrison.

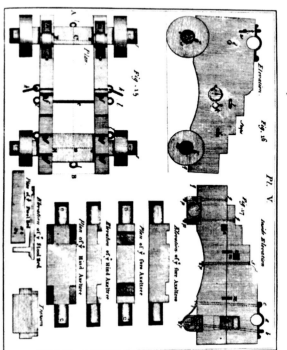

FIGURE 28. Garrison carriage. J. Muller, A Treatise of Artillery.

balls on a flat trajectory. The largest guns at Fort Mackinac between 1780 and 1796 were "six-pounders"—weapons that fired an iron ball weighing six pounds. Besides six-pounders, there were small 1/2 pounders, firing a ball of that weight. Guns were also able to fire anti-personnel shot called "grapeshot." Grapeshot was composed of a number of small iron balls that, when fired, acted much like scatter shot and could be extremely effective at close range against attackers trying to enter the fort. Guns were loaded from the muzzle (as was all artillery at this time). The larger guns were mounted on a carriage, either a two-wheeled field carriage or a four-wheeled garrison carriage.

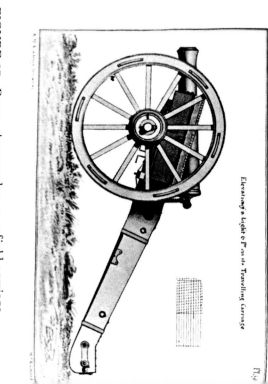

FIGURE 27. Brass six-pounder on a field carriage. J. Muller, A Treatise of Artillery.

There was one small brass mortar at Fort Mackinac during this period, its bore measuring 4 2/5'' in diameter. This type of small mortar was known as a "coehorn" and was mounted on a solid bed of wood. Several men could move it with relative ease for short distances and the very high trajectory possible with this weapon allowed shells to be dropped behind obstacles.

The last category of artillery at Fort Mackinac included "wall pieces." While not bonafide artillery, they were oversized muskets, mounted in a yoke like a swivel gun and used for anti-personnel fire.

When the British garrison of Fort Michilimackinac moved to Mackinac Island in 1781, they brought the weapons of the former post with them. In March, 1780, these guns numbered: [151]

2 Iron six-pounders
2 Brass six-pounders
4 Brass ambuzettes (swivels)
1 Brass 4 2/5'' mortar
2 wall pieces

All of these weapons were removed to the new Fort Mackinac except two of the ambuzettes. Although these two guns continued to be carried on Fort Mackinac's inventory, they were in fact mounted on board the sloop "Felicity."

A year later, the artillery at the post had been bolstered by the addition of three iron 1/2-pounders and two iron 3 1/2'' howitzers (possibly mortars). The fort's gun carriages seem to have been in poor shape, however, as there were only three carriages for four six-pounders and one serviceable carriage for the 1/2-pounders (at this point these small guns seem to have been mounted, at least in part, on garrison carriages). [152]

In March, 1782, there was one more iron 1/2-pounder and the gun carriage problem seems to have been largely alleviated, though there was still a shortage of carriages for the 1/2-pounders. [153]

The last artillery return we have for Fort Mackinac for the 1780s is dated 10 August 1783 and shows: [154]

2 Iron six-pounders
2 Brass six-pounders
2 Iron 3 1/2'' howitzers
4 Iron 1/2-pounder swivels
4 Brass ambuzettes
1 Brass 4 2/5'' mortar

During the late 1780s, the composition of the artillery at Mackinac changed very little. Some additions were made, however, and on 1 January 1794 a return of artillery comprised: [155]

2 Iron six-pounders
2 Brass six-pounders
2 Iron 3 1/2'' howitzers

FIGURE 29. A contemporary illustration showing small mortars and guns mounted on field carriages. J. Muller, A Treatise of Artillery.

Both types were used at Fort Mackinac. The 1/2-pounders were commonly known as "swivels" and were usually mounted in a yoke, resembling an oarlock, and could be mounted right on a wall. Iron gun tubes were painted black by the British and field carriages were grey. [148] Brass gun tubes were unpainted.

Howitzers, which were much shorter than guns, were designed to throw an explosive shell at a higher angle than a gun and yet be more mobile than a mortar. The shell that was fired was a hollow sphere, filled with gunpowder, with a fuse in one side. The idea was to set the fuse so that the shell would explode just as it reached the target—a chancy proposition at best. Whether the weapons listed as howitzers at Fort Mackinac were true howitzers is open to doubt. They were very small, having a bore 3 1/2'' in diameter, and were made of iron, [149] a material not normally used for howitzers or mortars. Possibly they were mortars and were so listed in one return. [150] These "howitzers" were also apparently mounted on garrison carriages.

8 Iron ½-pounder swivels
2 Brass ½-pounder swivels (the old ambuzettes minus the two given to the "Fecility")
1 Brass 4 2/5" mortar

Several other returns for 1794 show the same weapons and this artillery was all removed by the British in 1796 when the Post of Mackinac was ceded to the Americans.

The guns of Fort Mackinac were the responsibility of members of a detachment of the *Royal Regiment of Artillery* stationed at that post. During the years of the American Revolution, this detachment was usually only two enlisted men. [136] In the event of an attack upon the fort, the infantrymen of the garrison would have had to man the guns, with the artilleryman acting as trained supervisors. During the late 1780s, the detachment was supplied by the *4th Battalion/Royal Regiment of Artillery* and the size of this detachment varied between one and seven men, the most common number being three. [157]

The 1790s and the increased tension between Britain and the United States, saw a substantial increase in the Royal Regiment of Artillery detachment at Fort Mackinac. These later detachments were commanded by a sergeant and normally numbered eight to ten men. In 1793 there was even a drummer of the Royal Artillery in garrison. [158] When the fort was evacuated by the British in 1796, the artillery detachment was made

up of one sergeant and seven rank and file. [159] After the British evacuation, nearly all of the Royal Regiment of Artillery in Canada was recalled to Quebec. [160]

The Royal Regiment of Artillery was administered by the Board of Ordnance, as was the Corps of Engineers. The pay for the artillery was similar to that of the infantry except that artillery privates made 1 shilling/day [161] as compared to

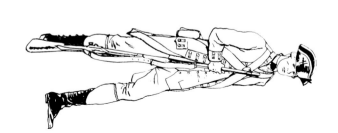

FIGURE 31. Private, Royal Regiment of Artillery.

FIGURE 30. The sloop *Felicity*, which was armed with two of Fort Mackinac's "ambuzettes." Painted by Homer Lynn.

white, rather than black leather. By the 1790s, the men of the *Royal Regiment of Artillery* also wore a white feather in their hats. [163]

THE MACKINAC MILITIA

Although the garrisons of Fort Mackinac from 1780 and 1796 were made up of red-coated regulars, there was another source of manpower upon which the commander of the fort was able to draw: the militia. Both Forts Mackinac and Michilimackinac had an adjacent town, and as in any other town in colonial America, the able-bodied men of these towns were required to join the militia.

The civilian population of the Straits of Mackinac area was largely of French-Canadian descent with a sprinkling of Englishmen and Scots who had come to participate in the fur trade. In 1780, all of the merchants and traders at the post were enrolled in the militia. [164] These men of the militia were not uniformed, but when called upon would wear their normal civilian clothing and probably

FIGURE 34. Private, Mackinac Militia.

carry their own weapons, though they might also be armed with spare weapons from the garrison. In March, 1790, it was suggested that some spare small arms be kept at Fort Mackinac for "such other people as may be occasionally thrown into the Fort for its defence & their own protection. . ." [165]

Probably the only occasion upon which the 1780-1796 militia was called out for the defense of Fort Mackinac came during the summer of 1784 when the regular garrison of the fort was suddenly reduced from about one hundred to roughly forty

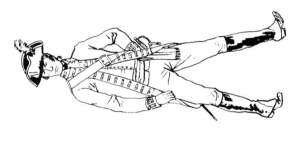

FIGURE 32. Sergeant, Royal Regiment of Artillery.

8 pence for an infantry private. The *Royal Regiment of Artillery* was grouped into four battalions of eight companies each [162] and the companies of the battalion serving in Canada were split up to provide detachments for the various posts.

The uniforms of the men of the *Royal Regiment of Artillery* were very similar in cut to those of the line infantry and also incorporated the minor style changes of the late 1780s. Artillerymen, however, wore a dark blue coat with lapels, collars, and cuffs of red. The turnbacks were red until 1782 when they were changed to white. Yellow tape was looped around the buttonholes and around the hat brim. The buttons were pewter for the men and gilt for officers and contained three cannonballs over three cannons, all within a shield. The breeches and waistcoats were white, and black gaiters, like those of the infantry were worn. The men also wore infantry-type crossbelts, although the cartridge boxes of the artillery differed from those of the infantry in that they were of

FIGURE 33. Officer's button, Royal Regiment of Artillery.

FIGURE 35. Fort St. Joseph which the British built when they left Mackinac. *Public Archives of Canada.*

FIGURE 36. Fort Mackinac, 1973.

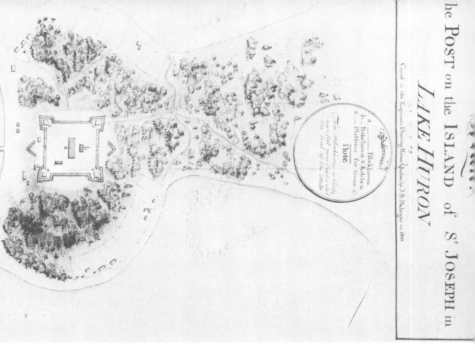

men. Captain Robertson felt that so small a garrison was inadequate to defend the post and he called upon the militia. Their duty was to mount "a Guard of Twenty men every night . . . and very cheerfully will continue so doing while there are a number of them sufficient for that purpose in the Traders Village." [166]

With the evacuation of Fort Mackinac in 1796, British militia organizations in the Straits of Mackinac area came to an end.

BRITISH OFFICERS AT FORT MACKINAC
1780-1796

The British Army detachments that served at Fort Mackinac were usually far under strength and this applied to the number of officers as well as to the number of enlisted men. A garrison of two companies of infantry at full strength should have had the following officers:

2 Captains
2 Lieutenants
2 Ensigns

A comparison of this with some of the garrison returns listed above will show the difference between this ideal and the actual complement of officers at Fort Mackinac at any one time. The companies themselves were under strength and, of course, would not have needed this many officers at all times. Officers were commonly granted leave of absence, were assigned to staff duty or were detached on special duty. Many officers remained in England while their regiments were overseas, and some probably never saw their units on active service.

The following list is a compilation of the British officers who served at Fort Mackinac between 1780 and 1796. It is nearly complete although some gaps have defied closing, especially those presented by the 65th Foot. The regiments are listed in numerical order with the dates, or approximate dates, of their duty at Fort Mackinac. The modern regimental designations of the units are given in parentheses. The officers are listed in alphabetical order under their units with the verifiable dates of their stays at Fort Mackinac.

5th Regiment of Foot (Royal Northumberland Fusileers) c. August 1790-1 July 1792

Captain Edward Charlton
Commanding Fort Mackinac c. August 1790-1 July 1792
Ensign James Mathew Hamilton
Winter 1791-1792 (probably c. August 1790-1 July 1792)
Ensign William Gleadowe
Winter 1791-1792 (probably c. August 1790-1 July 1792)
Lieutenant Benjamin Roche
Winter 1791-1792 (probably c. August 1790-1 July 1792)

8th or King's Regiment of Foot (King's Liverpool Regiment) 1774-6 August 1784

Lieutenant Thomas Bennett
August 1782
Lieutenant Robert Bounds Brooke, General's Company
Before 1780-September 1781
Lieutenant George Clowes, Granadier Company
Before 1780-September 1780
c. September 1782-21 April 1783
Ensign Philip R. Fry
c. September 1782-6 August 1784
Ensign John Robert McDonall (McDougall)
c. September 1780-c. September 1781
Lieutenant Daniel Mercer
Before 1780-August 1780
Captain John Mompesson
21 August 1780-20 August 1781
Ensign Robert Pollard (Lieutenant 13 September 1783)
c. September 1782-6 August 1784

24th Regiment of Foot (South Wales Borderers) 1 July 1792-1 September 1796

Ensign John Bromhead (Lieutenant 16 June 1795)
c. 1794-c. August 1796
Ensign Thomas Chamberlain (Lieutenant 3 September 1795)
c. 1794-95-c. August 1796
Captain William Doyle (Brevet Major 6 May 1795)
Commanding Fort Mackinac 1 July 1792-c. August 1796
Ensign Andrew Foster (Lieutenant 9 April 1794)
1 July 1792 ?-1 September 1796
Ensign John Carden Stronge (Lieutenant 12 March 1794)
1 July 1792?-1795?

34th Regiment of Foot (The Border Regiment) 4 August 1784-August 1786

Ensign George Dodsworth
4 August 1784-c. June 1785
Ensign Alexander McDonald
c. June 1785-August 1786?

44th Regiment of Foot (Essex Regiment)
No service at Fort Mackinac
Lieutenant Colonel Henry Hope
15 September 1782-21 September 1782

FIGURE 37. Officer, 8th Foot.

FIGURE 38. Officer, 65th Foot.

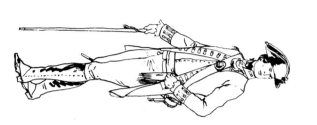

47th Regiment of Foot (The Loyal North Lancashire Regiment) 18 August 1781-24 October 1782

Captain Thomas Aubrey
18 August 1781-c. August 1782
Lieutenant Samuel Ford
18 August 1781-c. August 1782
Ensign Gustavus Hamilton (Lieutenant 1 April 1780*)
13 September 1781-c. August 1782
*First listed as a Lieutenant in 47th Foot return of 1 February 1782

53rd Regiment of Foot (King's Shropshire Light Infantry) August 1786-July 1788

Lieutenant William Houghton (Captain Lieutenant and Captain 24 September 1787)
August 1786-November 1787
Ensign Robert William Ottley
August 1786-July 1788
Lieutenant Daniel Robertson
c. June 1787-July 1788
Captain Thomas Scott
Commanding Fort Mackinac 15 June 1787-July 1788

2nd Battalion, 60th or Royal American Regiment of Foot (King's Royal Rifle Corps) c. 15 June 1789-c. August 1790

Ensign George Forneret (Lieutenant 9 December 1789)
c. 15 June 1789-c. August 1790
Lieutenant Gabriel Gordon
c. 15 June 1789-c. August 1790

Ensign Lewis Muller
c. 15 June 1789-c. August 1790
Captain John Parr
Commanding Fort Mackinac c. 15 June c. August 1790

65th Regiment of Foot (York and Lancaster Regiment) July 1788-c. 15 June 1789

Captain Alexander Malcolm
Commanding Fort Mackinac July 1788-c. 15 June 1789
No information on other officers of this regiment at Fort Mackinac.

1st Battalion, 84th or Royal Highland Emigrant Regiment of Foot (Disbanded 1784) 4 June 1780-c. July 1784

Captain Daniel Robertson
Commanding Fort Mackinac 1782-c. 15 June 1787
Ensign James Robertson
c. November 1782-c. July 1784
Captain Patrick Sinclair
Commanding Fort Mackinac 5 October 1779-18 September 1782

Royal Regiment of Artillery
Before 1780-c. August 1796

Lieutenant Christopher Meyers
August 1782

The Corps of Engineers

Practitioner Engineer and 2nd Lieutenant Richard Hockings
15 September 1782-c. October 1782
Captain Gother Mann
1788
Lieutenant Robert Pilkington*
1794?

*Possibly was never sent to Fort Mackinac.

ACKNOWLEDGEMENTS

The piecing together of the many details that allow the presentation of a description and history of Fort Mackinac's 18th century British garrisons would not have been possible without considerable assistance from a number of people and institutions. Chief among the former is Mr. René Chartrand, Military Curator of the National Historic Sites Service of Canada. Mr. Chartrand's expertise in research and reconstruction, his constructive criticism and his constant encouragement were indispensible to the completion of this work. Further encouragement and technical assistance came from Mr. Dirk Gringhuis, Curator of Exhibits of the Michigan State University Museum and illustrator of this booklet.

Documentation for this history came through the courtesy of the Public Archives of Canada in Ottawa, the William L. Clements Library in Ann Arbor, Michigan and the Libraries of the University of Michigan. To the helpful staffs of these three institutions I would like to express my gratitude.

NOTES

1. Lt. Governor Allured Clarke to Henry Dundas, 25 May 1793, *Michigan Pioneer and Historical Collections* (hereafter *MPHC*), XXIV, p. 539.

2. Edward E. Curtis, *The Organization of the British Army in the American Revolution* (New Haven: Yale University Press, 1926), p. 2.

3. *Ibid.*, pp. 4-5.

4. *Ibid.*, p. 67.

5. Return, 1 January 1781, Great Britain, Public Records Office, War Office 17, volume 1575 (hereafter WO 17 1575 etc.), p. 162. Microfilm Roll B-1588 at the Public Archives of Canada (hereafter PAC).

6. Cecil C. P. Lawson, *A History of the Uniforms of the British Army,* III (London: Norman Military Publications, 1961), pp. 109-114.

7. Curtis, *op. cit.*, p. 54.

8. *Ibid.*, p. 55.

9. *Ibid.*, pp. 22-23.

10. Petition of Two Companies of the 8th Foot, 30 July 1780, *MPHC*, IX, pp. 587-588.

11. Court Martial, 23 July 1790, *PAC*. C 930, pp. 71-75.

12. Curtis, *op. cit.*, p. 56.

13. *Ibid.*, p. 89.

14. Provision Return, 4 April 1780, *MPHC*, IX, p. 656.

15. Curtis, *op. cit.*, pp. 91-92.

16. Extracts from the Ste. Anne's Church Parish Register printed in Lt. Dwight L. Kelton, *Annals of Fort Mackinac* (Chicago: Fergus Printing Co., 1882), p. 63.

17. Barracks Returns, 24 April 1781, *MPHC*, X, p. 470 and 4 May 1796, *MPHC*, XXIII, pp. 340-41.

18. Parr to Harris, 6 June 1790, *PAC*. C 930, pp. 76-84.

19. Curtis, *op cit.*, pp. 91-92.

20. Mathews to Haldimand, 3 August 1787, *MPHC*, XX, pp. 289-291.

21. Donald R. Morris, *The Washing of the Spears* (New York: Simon & Schuster, 1965), p. 297.

22. *Ibid.*, p. 662.

23. Curtis, *op. cit.*, pp. 160-161.

24. Parr to Harris, 6 June 1790, *PAC*. C 930, pp. 76-84.

25. Return, 1 January 1780, WO 17 1574, p. 5, *PAC* Microfilm B-1588.

26. Petition of Two Companies of the 8th Foot, 30 July 1780, *MPHC*, IX, pp. 587-588.

27. Lawson, III, *op cit.*, pp. 109-114.

28. Sinclair Brehm, 29 October 1779, *MPHC*, IX, pp. 530-533.

29. DePeyster to Haldimand, 5 October 1779, *MPHC*, IX, p. 398.

30. Instructions to Patrick Sinclair, 1779, *MPHC*, IX, pp. 516-518.

31. Sinclair to Haldimand, 27 July 1779, *MPHC*, IX, p. 518.

32. Haldimand to DePeyster, 17 August 1779, *MPHC*, IX, p.364.

33. Haldimand to Sinclair, 20 August 1779, *MPHC*, IX, pp. 521-522.

34. Haldimand to MacLean, April (?) 1780, *MPHC*, XIX, p. 512.

35. *Army List* (London: War Office, 1781).

36. Haldimand to MacLean, 10 April 1780, *MPHC*, XIX, pp. 505-506.

37. Sinclair to Bolton, 4 June 1780, *MPHC*, XIX, pp. 529-530.

38. MacLean to Mathews, 14 September 1780, *MPHC*, XIX, pp. 573-574.

39. Haldimand to Sinclair, 12 September 1780, *MPHC*, IX, pp. 575-576.

40. Gage to MacLean, 12 June 1775, *PAC*. WO 28/4, p. 211.

41. Germain to Clinton, 1 April 1779, *PAC*. Microfilm roll M 848, Vol. 16, 1874, p. 113.

42. Gage to MacLean, 12 June 1775, *PAC*. WO 28/4, p. 211.

43. *Orderly Book. Royal Highland Emigrants. PAC. MG 23, K1, Vol. 21, 10 August 1777.*

44. MacLean to Haldimand, 27 November 1780, *PAC*. B 129, p. 189.

45. *Orderly Book. Royal Highland Emigrants.* 1 September 1776.

46. *Ibid.*, 15 February 1782.

47. Lt. Charles M. Lefferts, *Uniforms of the American, British, French and German Armies in the War of the American Revolution* (Old Greenwich, Conn.: WE Inc., reprint of 1926 edition), p. 193.

48. W. L. Calver and R. P. Bolton, *History Written with Pick and Shovel* (New York: New York Historical Society, 1950), p. 119.

49. MacLean to Haldimand, 27 November 1780, *PAC*. B 129, p. 189.

50. *Orderly Book. Royal Highland Emigrants.* 20 May 1782.

51. *Ibid.* 27 October 1782.

52. Petition of Two Companies of the 8th Foot, 30 July 1780, *MPHC*, IX, pp. 587-588.

53. Letter from Lt. Clowes, 23 August 1780, *MPHC*, IX, pp. 608-609.

54. Petition of Two Companies of the 8th Foot, 30 July 1780, *MPHC*, IX, pp. 587-588.

55. Mompesson to Haldimand, 22 August 1780, *MPHC*, IX, pp. 589-590.

56. Return, 1 February 1781, WO 17 1575, p. 38, *PAC* microfilm B-1588.

57. Mompesson to Haldimand, 22 August 1780, *MPHC*, IX, pp. 589-590.

58. Haldimand to Sinclair, 12 September 1780, *MPHC*, IX, pp. 575-576.

59. Letter from Sinclair, 31 July 1781, *MPHC*, X, pp. 502-503.

60. Mompesson to DePeyster, 28 April 1781, *MPHC*, IX, p. 632.

61. Haldimand to Powell, 24 June 1781, MPHC, XIX, pp. 643-644.

62. Ibid.

63. Aubrey to Haldimand, 30 July 1781, MPHC, X, p. 502.

64. Edwin O. Wood, Historic Mackinac, I (New York: Macmillan, 1918), p. 259. Extracts from the logbook of Capt. Alexander Harrow.

65. Ibid., p. 259.

66. Ibid., p. 260.

67. Return, WO 17/1575, p. 162, PAC microfilm B-1588.

68. H. C. Wylly, The Loyal North Lancashire Regiment, II (London: 1933), pp. 382, 384.

69. Return, 1 January 1782, WO 28/6, p. 104, PAC microfilm B-2864.

70. Powell to Haldimand, 17 August 1782, MPHC, XX, pp. 43-44.

71. Return, 1 September 1782, WO 17/1576, p. 155, PAC microfilm B-1589.

72. Return, 1 October 1782, WO 17/1576, p. 163, PAC microfilm B-1589.

73. Letter from Lt. Col. Hope, 21 September 1782, MPHC, X, p. 645.

74. Hope to Robertson, 20 September 1782, MPHC, X, pp. 638-640.

75. Engineer's Report, 20 September 1782, MPHC, X, pp. 642-645.

76. Hope to Robertson, 20 September 1782, MPHC, X, pp. 638-640.

77. Return, 24 December 1782, WO 28/6, p. 143, PAC microfilm B-2864.

78. Robertson to Brehm, 6 July 1783, MPHC, XI, pp. 373-374.

79. DePeyster to Haldimand, 15 July 1783, MPHC, XX, pp. 142-143.

80. Returns, 1 April to 1 July 1783, WO 17/1577, pp. 84, 107, 132, 155, PAC microfilm B-1589.

81. Specht to Haldimand, 7 October 1782, MPHC, XX, p. 63.

82. Original coat of Lt. Jeremiah French owned by his descendents in Cornwall, Ontario. Also a portrait of Samuel Mackay in the collections of the Musee National du Quebec, catalogue number A-54 282 d.

83. Calver & Bolton, op. cit., p. 129.

84. Return, 1 January 1784, WO 17/1578, p. 3, PAC microfilm B-1590.

85. Return, 1 February 1784, MPHC, XX, p. 213.

86. Haldimand to Robertson, 6 May 1784, MPHC, XI, pp. 226-227.

87. Robertson to Haldimand, 10 June 1784, MPHC, XI, pp. 415-416.

88. Ibid.

89. Mathews to Robertson, 12 August 1784, MPHC, XI, pp. 244-245.

90. Haldimand to Robertson, 29 March 1784, MPHC, XX, pp. 216-217.

91. Haldimand to Robertson, 29 March 1784, MPHC, XX, p. 216.

92. Robertson to Haldimand, 10 June 1784, MPHC, XI, pp. 415-416.

93. Robertson to Haldimand, 26 June 1784, MPHC, XI, pp. 419-420.

94. DePeyster to Haldimand, 28 June 1784, MPHC, XX, p. 235.

95. Return, 1 July 1784, WO 17/1578, p. 112, PAC microfilm B-1590.

96. Robertson to Haldimand, 5 August 1784, MPHC, XI, p. 442.

97. Thomas Hughes, A Journal by Thomas Hughes (Port Washington, N.Y.: Kennikat Press, 1947), p. 141.

98. Ibid., p. 141.

99. Return, 1 September 1784, WO 17/1578, p. 150, PAC microfilm B-1590.

100. Charles H. Stewart, The Service of British Regiments in Canada and North America (Ottawa: Department of National Defense Library, 1964), p. 179.

101. Lawson, III, op. cit., p. 119.

102. Ibid., pp. 109-114.

103. Mathews to Robertson, 4 September 1784, MPHC, XX, op. cit., p. 253.

104. Return, 1 May 1785, WO 17/1579, p. 66, PAC microfilm B-1590.

105. Return, 1 June 1785, WO 17/1579, pp. 72-73, PAC microfilm B-1590.

106. Return, 24 June 1785, WO 17/1579, p. 80, PAC microfilm B-1590.

107. Return, 1 July 1785, WO 17/1579, pp. 93ff, PAC microfilm B-1590.

108. Return, 1 September 1785, WO 17/1579, pp. 115ff, PAC microfilm B-1590.

109. Stewart, op. cit., p. 237.

110. Hughes, op. cit.

111. Ibid., p. 157.

112. Stewart, op. cit., p. 179.

113. Calver & Bolton, op. cit., p. 114.

114. Lawson, III, op. cit., pp. 109-114.

115. Return, 24 December 1786, WO 17/1498, pp. 24-25, PAC microfilm B-1567.

116. Mathews to Haldimand, 3 August 1787, MPHC, XX, pp. 286-91.

117. Wood, op. cit., pp. 584-585.

118. Army List (London: War Office, 1794).

119. Proceedings of a Court of Inquiry, 30 June 1788, MPHC, XI, p. 562.

120. Robertson to Mathews, 9 March 1784, MPHC, XI, pp. 406-407.

121. Return, 1 November 1787, MPHC, XI, pp. 508-509.

122. Mathews to Haldimand, 24 October 1788, MPHC, XX, pp. 294-295.

123. Hughes, op. cit. p. 168.

124. Ibid., p. 141.

125. Calver & Bolton, op. cit., p. 116.

126. Parr to Harris, 6 June 1790, PAC, C 930, pp. 76-84.

127. Stewart, op. cit., pp. 258-259.

128. Ibid., pp. 258-259.

129. George S. May (ed.), The Doctor's Secret Journal (Mackinac Island: Mackinac Island State Park Commission, 1960), p. 46.

130. Lewis W. G. Butler, The Annals of the King's Royal Rifle Corps (London: John Murray, 1913), Appendix pp. 6-7.

131. Mann's Report, 6 December 1788, MPHC, XII, pp. 30-37.

132. H. M. Walker, A History of the Northumberland Fusileers, 1674-1902 (London: 1919), p. 205.

133. Stewart, *op. cit.* p. 90.
134. Lawson. III. *op. cit.*. p. 96.
135. Return. 25 September 1792. *PAC*. C 930. p.3.
136. Lawson. III. *op. cit.*, pp. 109-114.
137. Return. 7 August 1795. *MPHC*. XXV. p. 93.
138. *Army List* (London: War Office. 1796).
139. Beckwith to Simcoe. 4 April 1796. *MPHC*. XXV. p. 114.
140. Beckwith's Evacuation Order. 1 June 1796. *MPHC*. XXV. pp. 120-121.
141. Duggan to Chew. 14 June 1796. *MPHC*. XII. p. 236.
142. Beckwith to the Duke of Portland. 5 July 1796. *MPHC*. XXV. p. 28.
143. Russell to Prescott. 29 August 1796. *MPHC*. XXV. pp. 129-130.
144. Selby to Chew. 13-16 August 1796. *MPHC*. XII. pp. 249-250.
145. *Fort Mackinac Orderly Book* in the collection of the West Point Museum. entry of 1 September 1796. p. 3.
146. Russell to the Duke of Portland. 6 August 1796. *MPHC*. XXV. p. 129.
147. Order for Evacuating Posts. 2 June 1796. *MPHC*. XXV. p. 121.
148. Harold L. Peterson. *Round Shot and Rammers* (Harrisburg, Pa.: Stackpole Books. 1969). p. 45.
149. Ordnance Return. 1 January 1794. *MPHC*. XII. p. 103.
150. Ordnance Return. 10 August 1783. *MPHC*. XX. p. 163.
151. Ordnance Return. 31 March 1780. *MPHC*. X. pp. 388-389.
152. Ordnance Return. 31 March 1781. *MPHC*. X. pp. 460-461.
153. Ordnance Return. 31 March 1782. *MPHC*. X. pp. 562-563.
154. Ordnance Return. 10 August 1783. *MPHC*. XX. p. 163.
155. Ordnance Return. 1 January 1794. *MPHC*. XII. p. 103.
156. Returns. 1780-1783. WO 17. *PAC* microfilm B-1588.
157. Returns. 1784-1787. WO 17. *PAC* mocrofilm B-1590.
158. Return. September 1793. *MPHC*. XXIV. pp. 606-607.
159. Return. 1 August 1796. *MPHC*. XXV. p. 128.
160. Beckwith to Simcoe. 4 April 1796. *MPHC*. XXV. p. 114.
161. Curtis. *op. cit.*. p. 159.
162. *Ibid.* p. 6.
163. Cecil C. P. Lawson. *A History of the Uniforms of the British Army. IV* (London: Norman Military Publications. 1966). p. 68.
164. Memorial of Merchants and Traders of Michilimackinac. 27 April 1780. *MPHC*. IX. pp. 549-550.
165. Mann's Report. 15 March 1790. *MPHC*. XXIII. p. 375.
166. Robertson to Haldimand. 5 August 1784. *MPHC*. XI. p. 442.

BIBLIOGRAPHY

British Army Lists. London: War Office, 1780-1796.

Butler, Lewis W. G. *The Annals of the King's Royal Rifle Corps*. London: John Murray, 1913.

Calver, W. L. and Bolton, R. P. *History Written with Pick and Shovel*. New York: New York Historical Society, 1950.

Curtis, Edward E. *The Organization of the British Army in the American Revolution*. New Haven: Yale University Press, 1926.

Fort Mackinac Orderly Book (1796-1798), original in the collection of the West Point Museum.

Hughes, Thomas. *A Journal by Thomas Hughes*. Port Washington, N.Y.: Kennikat Press, 1947.

Kelton, Lt. Dwight L. *Annals of Fort Mackinac*. Chicago: Fergus Printing Co., 1882.

Lawson, Cecil C. P. *A History of the Uniforms of the British Army*. III. London: Norman Military Publications, 1961.

Lawson, Cecil C. P. *A History of the Uniforms of the British Army*. IV. London: Norman Military Publications, 1966.

Lefferts, Lt. Charles M. *Uniforms of the American, British, French and German Armies in the War of the American Revolution*. Old Greenwich, Conn.: WE Inc., reprint of original 1926 edition.

May, George S. (ed.). *The Doctor's Secret Journal*. Mackinac Island: Mackinac Island State Park Commission, 1960.

Peterson, Harold L. *Round Shot and Rammers*. Harrisburg, Pa.: Stackpole Books, 1969.

Public Archives of Canada. "C" series papers.

Public Archives of Canada. Great Britain Public Records Office, War Office 17, volume 1498, *PAC* microfilm reel B-1567.

Public Archives of Canada. Great Britain, Public Records Office. War Office 17, volumes 1575-1579, *PAC* mocrofilm reels B-1588 through B-1590.

Public Archives of Canada. Great Britain, Public Records Office. War Office 28, volume 6, *PAC* microfilm reel B-2864.

Michigan Pioneer and Historical Collections, volumes IX-XII, XIX, XX, XXIII and XXV.

Stewart, Charles H. *The Service of British Regiments in Canada and North America*. Ottawa: Department of National Defense Library, 1964.

Walter, H. M. *A History of the Northumberland Fusileers. 1674-1902*. London, 1919.

Wood, Edwin O. *Historic Mackinac*. New York: Macmillan, 1918.

Wylly, H. C. *The Loyal North Lancashire Regiment*. London, Royal United Service Institution, 1933.

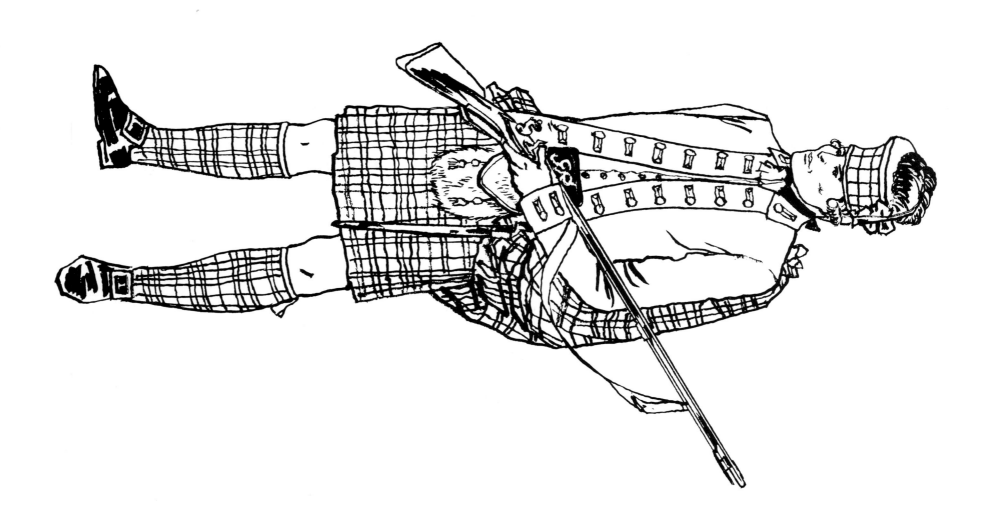